Or Did You Ever See The Other Side?

# Or Did You Ever
# See
# The Other
# Side?

Poems by

## Hedy Habra

**Press 53**
——•——
Winston-Salem

Press 53, LLC
PO Box 30314
Winston-Salem, NC 27130

First Edition

Cover art, "Woman, Lotus & Crane"
Copyright © 2020 by Hedy Habra

Cover design by Paul Sizer
paulsizer.com

Library of Congress Control Number
2023945266

ISBN 978-1-950413-69-0

*To my mother Henriette*
*who instilled in me her passion for art*

# Acknowledgments

The author thanks the editors of the publications where these poems first appeared, occasionally in different form:

*About Place Journal: Dignity as an Endangered Species,* "Or Have You Ever Noticed Erasure Patterns Within Fractals?"

*Axon: Creative Explorations,* "Or Aren't Words Worthless, Oftentimes Said & Forgotten, Written & Erased?" "Or Did You Think I'd Never Find The Way Out?"

*The Bitter Oleander,* "Or Did You Ever See The Other Side Of Things?" "Or How Can We Ever Cut Down To The Bare Essentials?" "Or How Long Do You Think She Could Keep It Up Without Falling?" "Or How With Each Dream She'd Feel Closer To The Receding Shoreline?" "Or What's In An Inverted Image?"

*Blue Fifth Review,* "Or What Did You Expect, An Eternal Status Quo?"

*California Quarterly,* "Or Did You Think Crushed Hopes Couldn't Reawaken?" "Or What Do You Learn When You Face Only Blue?" "Or Would It Have Made A Difference, Had I Known?"

*Cider Press Review,* "Or When Brushstrokes Dance In Concentric Circles"

*Connotation Press,* "Or Can't You See What We've Become Through The Half-Open Door?"

*Cordite Poetry Review,* "Or Did You Really Think It Was The Path Of No Return?"

*Cutthroat: A Journal of the Arts,* "Or Could I Finally Be Allowed To Leave My Analyst?" "Or How I Still Turn My Turkish Coffee Cup Upside Down"

*Feral: A Journal of Poetry and Art,* "Or How Did We Mend Failings With Golden Threads?"

*Fifth Wednesday Journal,* "Or Weren't You Ever Told That Nothing Comes Out Of Nothing?" "Or Why Do I Fast-Forward Lovers' Encounters On TV Shows?"

*Gargoyle,* "Or Don't Be Fooled By Her Self-Righteousness" "Or Don't You Ever Offer Yourself As A Main Course," "Or Don't We Often Need An *Allegro Ma Non Troppo?*" "Or How Could He Ever Win The Heart Of Any Woman?"

*Ghost Town,* "Or Do We Ever Learn To Find The Key To Our Own Scribbling?"

*The High Window,* "Or Can't You Hear The Harshness Of Her Breath?" "Or Who Would Have Expected Us To Leave That Way?"

*Impspired,* "Or How Could I Find My Way In Suspension In Midst Of A Clearing?" "Or How Do You Think We Came To Be Stranded In That No-Man's-Land?" "Or What If You Could Overhear Our Hushed Voices?"

*Knot Magazine,* "Or What Did You Think Would Happen After You Were Gone?"

*Live Encounters,* "Or Had She Told Him, Would He Have Understood?" "Or Have You Ever Heard Of A Cipher Even Freud Couldn't Elucidate?" "Or How Can Woven Whispers Be Deciphered?" "Or What If Scars Would Suddenly Become Translucent?"

*The MacGuffin,* "Or Can't You See That We Want Our Voices To Be Heard?" "Or How Did I Even Think I'd Make It Back In Time For Class?"

*The MacQueen's Quinterly,* "Or Call Me A Hoarder If You Will But Try To Understand"

*The Mantle,* "Or What Does A Tree Know About Aging?"

*MockingHeart Review,* "Or Didn't She Tell You She's Been A Mother For Too Long?" "Or Didn't You Know It's In That Opening & Closing That We Exist?" "Or How Do You Keep Track Of All The Keys You Once Owned?" "Or What If She Imagined He Loved Her Just That Once?" "Or Weren't We Always Told To Remove Our Makeup At Night?"

*The Night Heron Barks,* "Or Am I Or Am I Not A Knot Of Contradictions?"

*On The Seawall,* "Or Can't You See How They All Stare At Us Even The Birds Resting On Their Hands?" "Or What Else Could We Do But Raise Our Hands?"

*Panoplyzine Review,* "Isn't The Cat The Only Sensible Being In That Painting?"

*Pirene's Fountain,* "Or What If They Could Hear Each Other's Heartbeat?" "Or What Is Life If Not A Constant Carving Of Oneself?"

*Poetic Diversity: The Litzine of Los Angeles,* "Or What I Really Do When You Think I'm Knitting"

*The Opiate,* "Or How A Lover's Skin Shivers Like Moonlight Over Water"

*Peacock Journal,* "Or Do Memories Go Through Our Children Like Thread Through A Needle?" "Or How Could We Ever Be Able To Resist Such Likeness?"

*Riggwelter,* "Or Could There Ever Be Rainbows In Midst Of A Storm?" "Or How Did You Think She'd Rehearse Her Own Flight?"

*Rusted Radishes,* "Or Did You Ever Wonder What It's Like To Have Hot Flashes?"

*SLANT: A Journal of Poetry,* "Or Little Do You Know How A Bird's Song Rises," "Can't You See How We're Weaving Ourselves Tight?"

*Sukoon,* "Or Would She Ever Shed Her Many Faces?"

*Third Wednesday Journal,* "Or Have You Ever Wondered Why She Is Looking Back?"

*Tiferet Journal,* "Or What If She'd Chosen To Drown In A River Of Down?"

*Valparaiso Poetry Review,* "Or What If One Could Overhear Words Hovering Over A Pond?" "Or Why Would Anyone Want To Draw A Keyhole?"

*World Literature Today,* "Or How Much Of Yourself Remains Within The Walls Of A Home?" "Or What's In A Bird's Song, Unraveled?"

Anthologies:

Singapore Bicentennial Anthology, *SEVEN HUNDRED LINES: A Crown of Found/Fount Sonnets,* Glass Lyre Press and Squircle Line Press, 2019, "Or What If They Could Only Coexist As An Artefact?"

*Ekphrastic Writing: A Guide to Visual-Art-Influenced Poetry, Fiction, and Nonfiction,* McFarland, 2020, "Or Didn't You Know That What You Really See Is Your Own Reflection?"

Poems Nominated for Best of the Net:

"Or Do Memories Go Through Our Children Like Thread Through A Needle? (*Peacock Journal*)

"Or What Does A Tree Know About Aging?" (*The Mantle*)

Prose poem nominated for Best Microfiction:

"Or How Could We Ever Be Able To Resist Such Likeness?" (*The Ekphrastic Review*)

Poems Nominated for the Pushcart Prize:

"Or Can't You See That We Want Our Voices To Be Heard?" (*The MacGuffin*)

"Or How Did You Think She'd Rehearse Her Own Flight?" (*Riggwelter*)

"Or How Do You Keep Track Of All The Keys You Once Owned?" (*MockingHeart Review*)

"Or How Much Of Yourself Remains Within The Walls Of A Home?" (*World Literature Today*)

"Or Weren't We Supposed To Remove Our Makeup At Night?" (*MockingHeart Review*)

"Or What Did You Think Would Happen After You Were Gone? (*Knot Magazine*)

"Or What's In A Bird's Song, Unraveled?" (*World Literature Today*)

"Or Would It Have Made A Difference, Had I Known?" (*Indelible*)

# Contents

III.

IV.

I.

## Or Did You Ever See The Other Side Of Things?

Seated at her table, her fingertips run over
      the knots where branches
            once grew, feel the crevices
of the aged oak's grain, its porous surface
      about to peel open

like the pages of a book. She watches wavy
      lines swirl and burls' eyes
            sprout in threadlike tendrils . . .
Does a tree feel pain in its phantom limbs?
      Could the table remember

the carpenter's hands that carved it with love,
      the many times it was stained
            and rubbed with oils, would
these hands erase the memory of trees
      pregnant with bird trills?

And what of the movement of her pen, her
      unanswered questions, the songs
            she sang to herself? A heavy
breath in the nape of her neck rarefies the air.
      The chair's damask fabric,

woven with fleur-de-lis disintegrates, scattering
      petals wet with tears. Her open scars
            exposed, she feels the pull
of a body against hers, her hunger unveiled as
      the moment recedes.

## Or What's In A Bird's Song, Unraveled?

All artists are night owls, she thinks, as circles grow wider
around her eyes. Eyelids lowered, her brush, *an extension of
her violin-shaped heart,* adds the last touches of blush to the
feathers' tips. She tries to remember the right words thrown
pell-mell in the folds of memory . . . *memory adds layers to
meaning* . . . wants to retrieve numbers and signs from slumber,
relive the initial moment, imagines how wingless molecules
rub against each other in the copper alembic.

All it takes is a double binding broken loose to find the right
combination: *only verbs are allowed. Aren't they the heart of a
sentence?* What of a wordless message as those from the heart
strung from the right chord? She holds iridium glasses to gather
light from stardust . . . *hoopoes, hummingbirds, kingfishers,
finches, sparrows, swallows, warblers, orioles* . . . she has lost
track of how many species flew in search of an answer, *each
bird carrying its own song,* from all corners of the earth.

Her wings aren't strong enough to cross the seven valleys. *She
needs to send an emissary to partake in the colloquy of birds.*
Barefoot, she steps over shades of silver dust strewn by shooting
stars, conjures up their broken light night after night. The original
formula . . . *lost since time immemorial* . . . led to confusing myths
such as people drowning in their own reflection or making love
to their own creation. *She knows the secret of the bird's song,* its
loops and roundness, but chooses silence, lets its wings flutter
through the open window. She will try again.

## Or What If One Could Overhear Words Hovering Over A Pond?

She loosely wraps a muslin around her
slender body, waves swirl in suspension
from head to toes as she dresses and undresses
in a rhythmic motion. You'd think
she's getting ready for a performance, but
mirrors are banned from her walls, their
shattered shards buried in small boxes stacked
on shelves, their dark lids gathering dust like
archived journals, each filled with forgotten
objects, mute messages, layers shed from her past.

Each time she tries to open a box, hesitant,
she sees her fractured self staring, keeps
the lid half open like a half-open notebook
lest she'd stumble on the tumult of empty
words, ellipses, mostly silence.
Each time she faces this startled look, she slowly
lowers the lid, won't let the voice utter the same
unsettling questions hovering over her dreams,
over her dilated pupils still like the satin surface
of a pond, won't let her repeat what she already knows.

# Or Could I Finally Be Allowed To Leave My Analyst?

I am leaving his office with my hair standing on end. No iPhone
at hand, or else that would have made a great selfie. I walk out
with a steady stride, tired of these useless sessions. After all, am I
not reconciled with my dark side? No more makeup to hide the
once-widening circles around my eyes: I'll let the gray show on my
temples, allow my electric hair to rise and curl at will, catching
sunlight and moonbeams in its spires. I don't need him anymore but
he doesn't seem to know it. There's still work to be done, he says,
wants me back over and over again. I have no more stories to tell,
no more foggy areas to recover, forge, and weld. Has he become
addicted to my voice, or does he see his own shadow reflected in my
dreams? See, this is the story of my life: analyzing instead of being
analyzed, entertaining instead of being entertained.

## Or Weren't We Always Told To Remove Our Makeup At Night?

On certain evenings when the sun turns ebony, my heart becomes an obsidian pendant hanging between my breasts, conjuring old lovers' touch, my newborn's avid lips. I can then freely perform, peeling off face after face the masks that haunted me all my life, each dangling from a strand of my graying hair, caught within a self-woven web of conflicting feelings brimming with sap and dew. I become a puppeteer pulling threads of time, braiding throbbing heartbeats with the stillness of empty silences. That's when I realize how much care was taken in recreating myself as though with stage makeup. Or else how could I have coped with the different roles allotted to me at every crossroad, each gilded with a false sense of free will?

# Or How Could We Ever Be Able To Resist Such Likeness?

Now we look like a stencil copy as though divided via parthenogenesis
or were aphids avid to reproduce ourselves we no longer face each
other yet strum in unison the chords of our ukulele stretch our legs
sideways in the same comforting position as though we'd lived
together for so long we'd slide under each other's skin can't get over
that older man who told the younger me that touching one's spouse
was the same as touching oneself and yet what's more magical
than touching another skin and now that we are finally together
on that wooden raft about to sail as though seated within a dream
daydreaming of sailing on yet another boat on each side of that
cerulean horizon as though a fragile skiff was drifting awaiting to
color our reel and carry us away I wonder why the need for illusions if
we know the emptiness of words we might as well have concocted our
stories time after time yet still stumble over the same pebbles unlike
animals who never fall twice into the same trap our dulled senses
might not be able to resist such likeness our hair flowing in the breeze
in feathery strokes I feel that you are my mirror image and no longer
like what I see.

## Or Don't You Ever Offer Yourself As A Main Course

Wrapped in your finest lace, long curls loose, you sit by the table
set for two, decorated with the utmost care, the same care it took to
apply blush and eye shadow. The wind blows rusty leaves through the
open door, teases the flame of the flickering candle, its life half spent.
The cat has been in and out, tirelessly chasing the leaves littering the
hardwood floor. You think of the odds of writing a story in which he'd
grow tall, take a seat, share your candlelight dinner.

Eyes wide open, you stare at the flame, the only source of light; it
seems to rise, stretch and remain still at the same time, casting a
golden glow, morphs into an array of fluid shapes invading the room.
Behind you, a hand emerges from the heavy folds of the wavering
drapes, a hand, a replica of yours, reaches out, holds on firmly to your
wrist. Fingertips singe your skin, warn you of the times you've waited
in vain, wearing his favorite perfume. You hear your mother's voice
deafened, crossing that liminal space that fades away day by day.

# Or How Could He Ever Win The Heart Of Any Woman?

She shuffled seasons at will, carpeted her floors with grass and wildflowers, picked the first man who showed her a spark of kindness and carved his heart in her own image. Words danced in vibrant hues over the pages of her diary, giving life to a silhouette hovering in half tones in midst of the grisaille. With an empty stare, she'd sit for hours, see his shadow kneel in front of her, listen to his fading merman's song.

She'd redress his crossed eyes, bent shoulders, and slight limp, or else, how could he ever win the heart of any woman? She thought of *Beauty and the Beast,* although he was no beast and she was no beauty. Until the day she flung windows wide open, let gusts invade the rooms, let her skin bear the colors of dead leaves, and knew time had come to pull the thread, unravel the feelings spun around his heart.

## Or Don't Be Fooled By Her Self-Righteousness

If you could only see her when she slips into her sleek pajamas
and fights for hours with me, her alter ego, always dressed in
contrasting colors from head to toe. She favors the coolness of
seashell and ivory tones while my clothes are tainted with cravings,
the shades of fire and blood. That's why I can't stand her political
correctness though we've shared the same umbilical cord and most
of the time coexist harmoniously. Or is it because I usually fade
within her during the day, a replica she carries within, folded in
her pocket like a cardboard silhouette?

Only at night does she allow me to materialize and sit next to her.
Hours long we ask each other the sempiternal question: *Che vuoi?*
Maybe she yearns to accept me, the way a terminally ill patient
needs a blood transfusion or autologous stem cells? We coexist
in constant contradiction: one of us wants to swallow the whole
world, get up at dawn and run barefoot on the beach to catch the
first rays of sun while the other would rather lie down all day long
and watch the sun set.

# Or Am I Or Am I Not A Knot Of Contradictions?

Last night I woke up in angst. I thought my cat was scratching behind the closed door. It must have been a desperate critter scratching frenetically the surface, caught somewhere within the unfathomable layers wrapped around our home. Its tragic attempt at freedom left me terrified. I imagined the wall's plaster cracking open, giving place to another dimension from which a trapped bird or bat would fly, or was it another being immured for too long, striving to liberate itself as it sensed feathered nests in the back of the recliner's upholstery?

When I sit still for a while on my desk, I hear the growth of underground roots filling the interstices of tiles as though I were in an abandoned patio invaded by weeds or the ruins of an ancestral house. I am no longer alone, surrounded by reflections of my lengthening shadow rising over the walls. That's when I sense writing as a form of incantation. See, that's why I write, not to tell a story but to reconcile myself with the echoes of the tunes that keep singing within me like a haunting melody as the musical score becomes tridimensional, takes a life of its own, or is it just a variation on the same tune?

## Or How Much Of Yourself Remains Within The Walls Of A Home?

I wanted to dive into the troubled waters of forgotten memories, haunt the house of early emotions but found it empty. I wanted to find the lingering scent of jasmine where jasmine never grew, even if it wasn't spring. Unspoken words fall heavily on the kitchen tiles: a cascade of rough-edged syllables flood the floor. My chair is glued to the table, I'm trapped within clouds preventing me from seeing how the marsh grows wider, how walls collapse, spikes and bluish-green leaves crested with plumes line the edge of the water where glasswort blushes against sea lavender.

I'd run my fingers over the red, round stems, crush the purple petals under my teeth to release its essential oils. I can still see the russet tree's liquid mirroring, its gnarled roots that seem to reach up to the sky. Your body awakens each night under my touch, shortening the distance between my lips and your skin, until your body remembers, until the sky sinks into water, mist so thick, a hummingbird floats in minute droplets in suspension. I feel the current of the first kiss in my curls, our knees shaking.

## Or Didn't You Know It's In That Opening & Closing That We Exist?

At first sight, you might think we're these uprooted trees facing each other on that arched door, without touching, suspended, in stasis, our dreams unraveling a gilded ribbon around the branches, reaching out deep into our exposed verdigris roots. *Notice the double doorknob? It only opens when we turn the latch from the inside at the same time, at the same rhythm.* At first sight, that engraved wooden door might make you think of a tombstone for an old couple sleeping in separate rooms. When we both turn the latch, it's in that opening and closing that we exist, spinning on wheels under the triple moon crescent. For an instant, you might hear the fluttering of wings as we rise through spiraling staircases to heights never reached in our dreams.

## Or How Long Do You Think She Could Keep It Up Without Falling?

It's when the palm trees started swaying under the soaring wind that she held on tighter to the large olla resting on her shoulder, readjusting its base over the crowned woven cloth that kept it in place. She loved the cooling touch of fresh clay against her cheek as her stride espoused the rhythm of the feathered branches whirling like disheveled women in a maddened trance, oblivious to the rising lament calling for the evening prayer. Unlike other days, when she'd follow her daily route impervious to the male gaze that forced her to lower her eyelids, her eyes still filled with the sight of the horseman riding a nervous stallion alongside the shore, of a mare licking her foal in concentration, and the distant felucca gliding over the Nile's silvery mirror. The wind blew harder and as she strived to maintain her balance her steps got caught into an automatic dance. She sensed the ruffling and rustling of butterfly wings against her waist, around the mouth of the jug, and down her back. She no longer felt the weight on her shoulder unaware that her dreams were pouring out of the jug in a whirlwind of blue mist swirling into a shape-shifting jinn as though blue lotus petals had been steeped inside the well's clear water.

## Or How With Each Dream She'd Feel Closer To The Receding Shoreline

When first thing in the morning, I look into the mirror it's as though my nightmare were a mirror in which I'm about to drown: I see myself hanging onto a huge trunk submerged in the marsh. I keep trying night after night to cross the threshold separating me from the other shore, the one my mother's mother's great grandmother left bound in chains and like so many others kept staring aimlessly in the direction of her birthplace. Every night, I'm bound by my mother's recurrent dream, that must have been inbred or hereditary, passed on by word of mouth, or was it an imprint into the cell's memory that sent her visions of being chased by winding lianas lassoing the surface of the swamp, water rising in crested waves spitting up fish into the nearby cattails, trees bending ever lower to catch her with their low tangled branches, their eyes glowing in the dark? She knew there would be at least one path leading her to safety like those who had succeeded before her, although with each dream she'd feel closer to the receding shoreline, she'd hopelessly remain trapped in the wetlands, though at times, she'd wake up from the murky waters where she was left for dead holding onto a broken trunk singing her way out like a diva

II.

## Or How Do You Keep Track Of All The Keys You Once Owned?


keys to unlock one's buried memories
keys to the family cottage you had to sell
keys that once opened different-sized locks
keys that had to be changed after an effraction
keys that yearn for the doors they used to open
keys thrown into a deep well, still oozing blood
keys to the palaces King Farouk owned in Egypt
keys to learning how to deal with oneself and others
keys to the meaning of feelings that you kept losing
keys to the safes holding papers that ruled your lives
keys kept in a jewelry box that must have mattered once
keys, lost, forgotten or treasured as a possible come back
keys to the wrought-iron patio gate half-covered with jasmine
keys that opened the car door that led you straight to the beach
keys to dreams' horned and ivory gates that keep getting mixed up
keys meant to reach the heart of a man before he'd change the locks
keys you hold in your palm and run your fingers over and over again
keys to an old friend's house who once relied upon you to water her plants
keys passed on from generation to generation to reclaim the ancestral home
keys that you had to return to the hotel where you wished you'd spend a
                                                                    lifetime
keys to all the cars you've ever owned and led you through long-forgotten
                                                                crossroads
keys to the office you left carrying a cardboard box filled with what seemed
                                                                important
keys to the wooden-carved secretary your mother handed down to you that
                                                        held no secret to her
keys to the homes you kept leaving, from country to country, from one
                                                neighborhood to the next

## Or What's In An Inverted Image?

He often sails
at dawn
lassoes the sun
with a line
strung
with a constellation
of stars
throws rainbows
and slivers
of moon crescents
into
the ocean's depths
where
all frustrations lie
till layers
and layers of waves
echo
the colors of the rainbow

# Or What If She'd Chosen To Drown In A River Of Down?

Some want to drown in their dreams
or in amber drink, others in denial,
            whilst she thinks of a river
of clouds sweeping her high above, sinks

in a river of down suffocating—without
            wetting her auburn curls: yes, vanity
still prevails in such moments.

Is there something worth dying for,
she wonders? But maybe, just maybe,
            if you live long enough you may
cross the threshold of desire, its constantly

deferred lack, learn to yearn for sunshine,
            await the concert of birds.
Once upon the time, tempests took

hold of her heart. Chest tight, she withheld
her tears, realized she was never asked:
            "What do you really want?"
and lifted the veil off her face.

There comes a time when ashes
            become so cold you can no longer
remember a fire was ever started.

There comes a time when you know
you've lost your moisture
            and if you dream of drowning
even drowning should be dry.

# Or What Did You Expect, An Eternal Status Quo?

At first sight, one might think of a table set for dinner with Poseidon, decorated with starfish and corals. But these must be the remnants of Tantalus's feast, eroded by centuries of retelling, and since no one gave it an end, let me tell you what really happened: with time, these fruits were covered with a green fur of algae and moss, starfish nested in their pores, filled every interstice.

Gods grew tired of holding a grudge, weary of the elusive offerings that kept alive his unforgivable offense. Can you imagine the inconceivable attempt to have them ingest the flesh of their flesh? One morning, they decided to dissolve in deep blue the memory of every sign of life reminiscent of former dissidence. They didn't bother to erase footsteps or leftovers, leaving traces for bards to reconstruct the story of those who would dare sit at this same table, transformed into a coral reef.

It's all left for us to admire and write about! Watch what fills this amphora, jug and agate glass bowls: soft blue-green and purple clouds. These iridescent vessels, no longer bearing pulpous fruits, have become artifacts, what you would now call a ready-made, more beautiful than the sunken Phoenician treasures displayed at the Met.

# Or What Does A Tree Know About Aging?

You'd think me impervious
    to my surroundings
        little do you know
of my inner struggles
    anchored deeply
        in strata swollen
roots protruding
    petrified pillows
        bearing traces
of endless processions
    insects' footprints
        antennae probing
every crevice
    the slightest orifice
        a witness to fallen
leaves transparent like lace
    skeletal nervures turned
        into butterfly's wings
decaying flesh
    too many skins shed
        layers and layers
of debris pelage encrusted
    inside fissures
        muffled voices
instants when time rests
    sounds of crackling
        pine needles under
footsteps resin sticking
    onto fingers, sighs
        in stark darkness
age is often equated
    with wisdom
        I equate it
with survival.

# Or Weren't You Ever Told That Nothing Comes Out Of Nothing?

*A black, E white, I red, U green, O blue: vowels,*
*I shall tell, one day, of your mysterious origins*
—Arthur Rimbaud

Rimbaud colored letters in his Alchemy of words,
turned silences and nights into verse.
I am now coloring notes just for you,
out of my deferred longings
out of the dregs of deepest sadness,
out of my shattered  hopes.

Let's string notes like beads, form
an invisible swirling strip
heavy with rhythm.
Let this musical phrase coil around trees
like a gilded ribbon
around every home we have ever lived in,
every threshold
we have ever crossed.

See how colors arise from heartbeats
despite distances,
how echoes resonate, giving life to inaudible drums
through closed doors and windows,
through stonewalls,
through walls of indifference,
walls of ignorance,
walls of fear and prejudice,
walls constantly hollowed,
by the piercing humming,

as easily as a silken thread
weaving us all together,
wherever we are, attentive to its tune.

# Or Little Do You Know How A Bird's Song Rises

When I set out to paint a tree
a bird's song rises
from each branching stem
sings its way
into a refugee tent
conjuring the warmth
of a mother's kiss
a song sinking into the mud
a song aching for cold hands
a song bleeding like sore soles
a song to erase the rising fumes
a song to protect from crumbling walls
a song for the comfort of an evening meal
*a song bleached*
*a song deafened*
*a song for those fallen*
*a song for those in pain*
a song ruffled by the wind
a song for those left behind
a song muffled by baby's cries
a song beating inside the chest
a song soothing an infant's dry lips
a song leaking from swollen nipples
*a song bleached*
*a song deafened*
*a song for those fallen*
*a song for those in pain*
a song lost in translation
a song in a new alphabet
a song to dig deep trenches
a song calling for clean sheets
a song to forget whistling bullets
a song to silence the voice of thunder

# Or Could There Ever Be Rainbows In Midst Of A Storm?

Men and women
wearing rainbows
ready to ride waves
as though they
were clouds
beneath
a magic carpet

hands raised
they look in the same
direction
there must be
a benevolent God
guiding the fragile skiff
to safety

      *only one face looks back*
*making sure*
      *that instant is alive*

oblivious to thirst
oblivious to hunger
oblivious to sunburn
oblivious to brine
dripping over scorched skin

as long as the boat
is floating they
stick together
forming the same
rainbow defying
the tall waves
the angry scum

     *only one face looks back*
*making sure*
      *the scene is recorded*

## Or What Else Could We Do But Raise Our Hands?

What of the feeling of sinking
                        whether in water or quicksand
                when a tidal surge or a sandstorm
engulf streets, when silt, dust,
                        shards, erase boundaries, words
                break down, and scattered letters
run wild in search of meaning

                we raise our hands

                        when the earth shakes, when
                institutions falter, whether it is
        a fault line, an explosion,
or an unforgivable negligence,
                when heirlooms and artworks bleed
        to death, their remains floating,
                        when we need to start from scratch,

                we raise our hands

when pine needles whisper
                        hopelessly trying to reach
                an empathetic ear or heart
when rooted underground veins
                        shiver in inaudible speech,
                when fragmented words rant,
stop conveying meaning

                we raise our hands

when rivers and waterfalls
                    darken, suffused with harmful
          dejections, debris and waste,
when tired fish no longer procreate,
                    when trees yearn for their
          birthright, remembering their
                              original sap, and fruits wither

          we raise our hands

when a knotted hand shivers
                    for lack of care and medicine
          when trust is buried under deceit
when windows shatter and buildings
                    stand naked, when firemen are thrown
          into an unfathomable abyss

          we raise our hands in prayer
               we raise our hands in anger
                    we raise our hands,
                         we raise our
                              we raise
                                   we

# Or Did You Think Crushed Hopes Couldn't Reawaken?

Imagine a feathered blown-glass
        sculpture falling from its pedestal,
                its opalescent fragments
        scintillating a thousand suns.
                        Imagine deft fingers placing
        tesserae after tesserae
                stretching an unending mosaic
        breathing with renewed hopes
under fingertips' beating pulse
        as though these fingers
                recomposed shredded documents
into different new meanings.
        Imagine how the firebird
                emerges spiraling, ruffling
        its feathers, follow
the undulating neck, wings ready
        to pulsate within restricted space,
                its spirit throbbing, about to soar.

# Or What Do You Learn When You Face Only Blue?

*Upon Visiting My Son for Christmas in Santa Barbara, CA*

How could one explain that need for blue
      as the sky merges with dense waters
pierced by whales spitting funnels of mist
          gasping for air like a cigar smoker choking
as cormorants' wings cut that blueness
      with dark, powerful strokes?

How could there be a need for blue
      if not for the saturation of winter grays
naked branches highlighted with a brush
          of greenish ochre the crispiness of oak leaves
covered with frost's confectioners' sugar
      or when one feels trapped under Michigan's

opaline sky like inside a Lalique crystal as though
      resting in one of the crystal coffins
Chinese legends deem necessary for an immortal's
          reincarnation? And yet I love mornings following
a snow storm, marvel at every twig's
      iridescence, the sun's rays oscillating

through each minute lens. And would hibernating insects
      sense the throbbing of roots beneath
the frozen blanket awaiting the right time to release
          sap to the tip of the branches curled inside
before unfurling tendrils' viridescent hues?
      What do you learn when you face only blue?

# Or How I Still Turn My Turkish Coffee Cup Upside Down

When I was single, mom, you used to bend over the dregs' configurations, conjuring up budding shapes, intricate encounters rising along the porcelain walls. You'd ask me to press my thumb inside the murky bottom to petrify an incipient evil eye. After I got married, how you laughed at me: *you already know your luck!* We could foresee trips, reunions, question the cornucopia of inked silhouettes, hollowed tree trunks, animals whispering messages or bearing pearls in their mouths. After you were gone, twenty years ago, I have been reading my own luck every day, projecting my hopes and calming my fears. During the past ninety days at home I've maintained the ritual, defying all odds. What am I hoping to find in the cup? I know I won't be able to travel to California to hold my son's first baby boy in my arms.

# Or How Do You Think We Came To Be Stranded In That No-Man's-Land?

when your mother is dying in a hospital and you can't hold her hand
when you are pacing from room to room yearning for a friendly voice
when museums' hallways are haunted by a few masked people
when you die a thousand times of longing because you can only see
your loved ones through a screen
when you know funerals must be solitary affairs and weddings
have become intimate
when you can't hug your grandchildren don't you inhabit a no-man's-
land designating others as persona non grata?
when you only need to review old sci-fi movies to realize how
their surrealness has swept into your own life
when deserted streets and avenues unfold over our screens
don't we feel stranded in an absurdist novel or maybe a hybrid painting
conceived by a collaboration between Kay Sage and her husband Yves
Tanguy within the setting of Dali's anamorphic landscapes and wouldn't
the ultimate construct translate into a movie fit for the times?
When Magritte's veiled lovers step out of the canvas reeking with repressed
sensuality and Abercrombie's touchless courtship seems natural aren't you
then convinced that life imitates art since these characters learned the notion
of physical distancing before it became the norm?

# Or How Can We Ever Cut Down To The Bare Essentials?

He kept retreating from room to room, feeling the weight of all the furniture and mementos staring at him like deceased relatives. It was as though the house wrapped layers of time around him, confining him inside a pod about to burst open. For a while he'd only use his bedroom and the kitchen. He eventually retreated to the sunroom. Its walls lined with bookshelves comforted him as he lay on the wicker couch opposite the bay window. He soon realized he needed fewer meals and only one change of clothes.

Feathers seemed to grow out of his bones, filling him with a desire to embrace the movements of the wind. He tried to get rid of plants, of his archived papers, of the photos that couldn't find their place in the abandoned albums. He sorted out the books he knew he'd never read or reread. Finally, the day came when unable to break all ties, he clung to his tabby, the photo of a woman, a purple-lipped cattleya, a few books, anything he could hide under his strong wings, slammed the door and left.

III.

# Or Call Me A Hoarder If You Will But Try To Understand

Each and every object in my drawers has a story of its own.
When I revisit the selves I once was, minute black silhouettes
Align themselves over the power lines of my mind as on a score
Until the outline of an alter ego irrupts, adding a silent note.

When I revisit the selves I once was, minute black silhouettes
Rub over every object's skin, absorbing smells and vibrations
Until the outline of an alter ego irrupts, adding a silent note
And would they engage in a dialogue in the utmost darkness?

Rub over every object's skin, absorbing smells and vibrations
Like the rosary stringed with pearls my mom loved so much
And would they engage in a dialogue in the utmost darkness
Map the vestibules of memory, run fingers over shining veins?

Like the rosary stringed with pearls my mom loved so much
Boxes of leftover yarn, her crocheted creations tucked into drawers
Map the vestibules of memory, run fingers over shining veins
Call it a bric-a-brac fit for those of us prone to engage in bricolage.

Boxes of leftover yarn, her crocheted creations tucked into drawers
A bleached sand dollar that might become your grandson's treasure.
Call it a bric-a-brac fit for those of us prone to engage in bricolage.
Nothing is what it seems, only the meaning invested in its arcane language

A bleached sand dollar that might become your grandson's treasure
And just the sight of a handwriting triggers the deepest emotions
Nothing is what it seems, only the meaning invested in its arcane language.
I keep digging as I become the archeologist of my own experience

# Or Can't You See That We Want Our Voices To Be Heard?

*A pantoum for unity وحدة after César Vallejo's "Masa"*

Women of all ages hair down or veiled speak in unison
We stand shoulder to shoulder in the streets of Lebanon
Want to be heard and seen from windows and on screens
We won't desist lest the puppeteers rewrite their script

We stand shoulder to shoulder in the streets of Lebanon
See how men and women of all faiths are holding hands
We won't desist lest the puppeteers rewrite their scripts
Stop pushing brother against brother sister against sister

See how men and women of all faiths are holding hands
Let's reclaim our land, merge our solitude into one وحدة
Stop pushing brother against brother sister against sister
Watch our five fingers form the hand controlling our lives

Let's reclaim our land, merge our solitude into one وحدة
We want you to hear our children's voices begging for change
Watch our five fingers form the hand controlling our lives
Let our trees bear fruits again why go where fruits ache for sun

We want you to hear our children's voices begging for change
Let them return from distant lands where flowers lost their scent
Let our trees bear fruits again why go where fruits ache for sun
Let's stand till the soles of our feet grow roots anchoring us

## Or Can't You See How They All Stare At Us Even The Birds Resting On Their Hands?

Packed against one another clothed in dreams
Upholding the flame of freedom for a mast
See how multicolored fish leap out around the hull
In quieted waters silvery fins quiver awaiting a net

Upholding the flame of freedom for a mast
Past and future fit into the wooden vessel
In quieted waters silvery fins quiver awaiting a net
While they rest under the shade of pregnant trees

Past and future fit into the wooden vessel
They are wearing Sunday clothes yet to be sewn
While they rest under the shade of pregnant trees
They sample ripened pomegranates and pink peaches

They are wearing Sunday clothes yet to be sewn
After fighting maddened waves for so long
They sample ripened pomegranates and pink peaches
They've slipped through the eye of a needle

After fighting maddened waves for so long
How sweet it is to emerge unscathed in extremis
They've slipped through the eye of a needle
Reaching a place where the wind is silent

How sweet it is to emerge unscathed in extremis
Future wraps itself around them in a colorful mantle
Reaching a place where the wind is silent
The cat slumbers as the restless dog rushes to the rooftop

# Or Would It Have Made A Difference, Had I Known?

Little did I know that when I'd wear my wedding gown
I'd be crossing a revolving door to a path of no return
At six I pricked my fingers with my needlepoint
Learning to be the best bride a man could wish for

I'd be crossing a revolving door to a path of no return
Away from clearings where I'd dip my feet into the stream
Learning to be the best bride a man could wish for
As I'd try not to burn myself with pots and pans

Away from clearings where I'd dip my feet into the stream
I bit my tongue to learn my mother-in-law's recipes
As I'd try not to burn myself with pots and pans
Little did I know how heavy unwanted weights could be

I bit my tongue to learn my mother-in-law's recipes
Felt my heart shrink year after year till it lost its beat
Little did I know how heavy unwanted weights could be
With greying hair, I still feel the need for a warm touch

Felt my heart shrink year after year till it lost its beat
Night after night I slip silently between the sheets
With greying hair, I still feel the need for a warm touch
Recapture an elusive smile in a face with receding features

# Or Did You Ever Wonder What It's Like To Have Hot Flashes?

Imagine a nebulous landscape covered with budding volcanoes
See yourself emerge from one of its peaks head heavy with slumber
Gasping in the rarefied air you enter a liminal space where unlucky few
Forever trapped past conception are condemned to parthenogenesis

See yourself emerge from one of its peaks head heavy with slumber
Think of your skin as a primed canvas permeable to imprints
Forever trapped past conception, condemned to parthenogenesis
See how the change of seasons leaves indelible marks all over your body

Think of your skin as a primed canvas, permeable to imprints,
You yearn for the sight of a veil billowing on a deserted deck's caravel
See how the change of seasons leaves indelible marks all over your body
Like the sfumato created by passing a candle over moist paper or canvas

You yearn for the sight of a veil billowing on a deserted deck's caravel
Suddenly a cooling current lassoes drifts unfurling into ashen flames
Like the sfumato created by passing a candle over moist paper or canvas
Or a haze hiding a palimpsest of thoughts carried by windswept fumes

# Or Isn't The Cat The Only Sensible Being In That Painting?

The woman's Medusa hair stands up on her head in ringlets
Though not electrified by the sudden backyard's lightning
Her men battle their way furiously through bending wheat
Golden braids sway in waves eager for the kiss of the scythe

Though not electrified by the sudden backyard's lightning
She kneads, stretches and folds the dough like an automaton
Golden braids sway in waves eager for the kiss of the scythe
While they fulfill their wish to be the Sisyphus of the field

*The cat's calls remain unheard as he shrieks at the sight of the felled tree*

She kneads, stretches and folds the dough like an automaton
In defiance, she will only use packaged flour from the store
While they fulfill their wish to be the Sisyphus of the field
The smell coming out of the pyre-like oven seals the sacrifice

In defiance, she will only use packaged flour from the store
They live in parallel universes rubbing against each other's bubble
The smell coming out of the pyre-like oven seals the sacrifice
Or is everyone about to explode in spontaneous combustion?

*Only the cat hears their unuttered words: will anyone listen to his warnings?*

# Or Can't You See How We're Weaving Ourselves Tight?

Didn't you think you'd soar high up when you wore a miniskirt?
I lowered my hemline, surrendering to ghost owls' hoots
Following the rhythm of my elder's everlasting refrains
When she visited the Louvre she wanted to wear her skin bare

I lowered my hemline, surrendering to ghost owls' hoots
Wore a key chain around my wrist that didn't open any doors
When she visited the Louvre she wanted to wear her skin bare
Chest open to the drifts of wind as she'd march with Delacroix's banner

Wore a key chain around my wrist that didn't open any doors
Afraid to face the black sun of Melancholy sung by Gerard de Nerval
Chest open to the drifts of wind as she'd march with Delacroix's banner
She enters the triple dance, a sarong loosely wrapped around her hips

Afraid to face the black sun of Melancholy sung by Gerard de Nerval
I conjure my younger self's steps eager to unlock the darkness
She enters the triple dance, a sarong loosely wrapped around her hips
The three of us dive into the emerald waters under the blackened sun

I conjure my younger self's steps eager to unlock the darkness
You didn't soar high up still unable to satisfy your hunger
The three of us dive into the emerald waters under the blackened sun
United at last in our quest for meaning, weaving ourselves tight

# Or How A Lover's Skin Shivers Like Moonlight Over Water

Let's dream of the full moon through transparent roofs
Deafened walls watch you sleepwalking with eyes wide open
Embrace this wake as sand awakened by dew at dawn
Follow the flame's glow as hours glide over prayer beads

Deafened walls watch you sleepwalking with eyes wide open
A lost *mobilis in mobili* rocked by the tide's ebb and flow
Follow the flame's glow as hours glide over prayer beads
Let's store worries in a drawer and throw the key away

A lost *mobilis in mobili* rocked by the tide's ebb and flow
Shake every speck of stardust from your hair and thoughts
Let's store worries in a drawer and throw the key away
Be happy you've just crossed one task out of a long list

Shake every speck of stardust from your hair and thoughts
Don't acknowledge yourself as an avatar of a higher self
Be happy you've just crossed one task out of a long list
Let's invert it all, climb the slightest beam of light

Don't acknowledge yourself as an avatar of a higher self
Draw your strength from a phoenix riding a tsunami
Let's invert it all, climb the slightest beam of light
See how a lover's skin shivers like moonlight over water

## Or Can't You See What We've Become Through The Half-Open Door?

We have dissolved into a scarce geometry, illusions erased line by line, and what is left is the tediousness of morning coffee ritual before sliding into invisible cubicles. Can't you see we have lost our shadow? We have vanished into straight lines and become an outline.

Only when we meet in that isolated place do our shapes appear to be formed as we once were. Sacred ashes come from the dust gathered under our soles on the long way here, in search for the mystery of an early evening bleeding in cobalt hues, the secrecy of empty walls on which to engrave our names, to shelter us from the passing of time.

We leave the door ajar, the half-open door casts a cone of light over the floor, an intrusive presence in the unlit room reaching us in the dark corner where we think we are secluded prisoners unable to escape the threshold of death, imagine our hands tied behind our backs reaching out only with an invented alphabet as an amulet to remember our time together.

All tales we tell ourselves, reinventing myths floating in incense, passageways to memory linked to the slightest touch as we submit to the painter's brush in this simulacrum of transgression.

# Or What If You Could Overhear Our Hushed Voices

At first glance, you can see that I'm not lying on the blue sofa,
nor hiding under it. But how about the open window framing
the white horse's head peeping into the empty room? Could I be
outside the canvas, listening behind walls?

Some might say that the meditative owl perched on the shelf
is my alter ego, my mirror image looking back at you,
or couldn't it rather be the horse? Now, if you were to enter
my dreams in search of a clue,

you might still not find me but you'll be able to hear me
talking to my divided selves watching over me like guardians.
Yet so much is left unsaid like in Chinese ink brush painting;
you know, those blank areas

similar to pauses in poetry? This is where the calligrapher's
brushstrokes form verses, beckoning you to add your own.
Picture me lying down on the aquamarine sofa, musing over
the space of desire. I sink into the velvet

upholstery as in a tailored cloud, see myself riding the wind,
a winged stallion oblivious to the monotonous raison d'être
of the wary owl. Could I be the moderator of their diatribes?
When my mother's sight was failing,

she would sit silently for hours, then, open up like a live
notebook enumerating aloud all of the to-do things while I'd
become part of a Xu Beihong ink-and-wash galloping horse,
hair flowing in the wind, the featherlike

equine mane caressing my face
till I'd face her absent look
swallowing life with every breath.

## Or Do Memories Go Through Our Children Like Thread Through A Needle?

There is a gap we do not see, that slips through
　　　　the folds of time, a tear in the fabric of passing on
　　　　　　　memories. Fallen leaves hide furrows carved by
raindrops. Could such tears be mended, embroidered
　　　　with colored threads to hide their seams?

*Should we teach our children the art of passing a thread through a needle?*

My mother used to draw patterns on linen tablecloths.
　　　　She planned one for each of her daughters' future home,
　　　　　　　seating up to twenty-four guests. They'd marvel
at the purple wisteria falling in clusters, wild vines circling
　　　　each plate, petals glistening with gilded thread.

*Don't the Chinese say we eat first with our eyes?*

Was there ever any doubt that we would get married?
　　　　When I turned fifteen, dreaming of travels and studies,
　　　　　　　she started her petit point tapestry as part of my
trousseau. I tried to dissuade her: what if I wouldn't care for
　　　　two Louis XIV chairs in the corner of my living room?

*You will appreciate it all when you're older, you'll see!*

She kept alive the movement of the needle, threading moth-resistant
　　　　wool that blossomed in magenta and fuchsia bouquets.
　　　　　　　Decades later, I can still see her eagerness in getting
them ready. They are now wrapped in silk paper in my cedar closet,
　　　　the leftover yarn rests in a box in the basement.

## Or Aren't Words Worthless, Oftentimes Said & Forgotten, Written & Erased?

We used newspapers to clean window panes when
I was growing up. With sheets crumpled up in balls
moistened with vinegar, we'd rub in circles till words
lost their lives, broken down into letters, ink fading
into erasures, signs reforming anew.

And what of the ritual cleaning and storing Persian
carpets for the long summers? The last step involved
lining them with newspapers soaked in turpentine.

We would kneel, two or three of us, depending
upon the size of the rug, and start rolling tightly,
in the shape of a log, like a *bras de Venus* cake,
rolling inch by inch, to avoid any trace of air
inviting moths to invade spaces, bite their way

into the handwoven wool. And did we ever glance
at any buried headlines, or worry about words receding,
their dye drowning within the meaning once conveyed?

And what of the fate of pages torn out of books,
never opened or abandoned volumes, forbidden
novels, put on the Index, or fallen into oblivion?
At school, the nuns would only lend us books
bearing an imprimatur seal or a nihil obstat.

The day my dad died they took me to my cousins' house.
I saw a book cover: a hairy-chested man in a striped pajama
bottom holding a redhead woman in a matching top.

That hardcover stained my mind with a taste of sin.
We never knew we were growing up in a cage,
until words themselves rebelled, burst out of rolled
rugs, discarded paper balls, recycling bins,
became flying doves unlocking doors.

Follow their flight through crystal clear windows,
so clean they'd vanish into thin air,

see them rest over flying carpets, refusing to fade
or be forgotten, stronger wings morphing

into fins, reaching out with their music to heights,
valleys and rivers where people thirst for the sound of letters.

# Or Didn't You Know That What You Really See Is Your Own Reflection?

Listen. Everyone thinks I've had it all, but let me tell you. Things aren't as they seem. Look at the pond's mirroring surface; it tricks you into thinking nothing perturbs its deeper layers, yet who knows how many mini tragedies unfold within its murky bottom? You say you wish you'd find a man like your dad. He was not the man you see now. It takes a lifetime. You need to slide stakes in slowly, overlook an occasional bending, praise the slightest effort.

I still recall that evening when I saw him through lowered blinds, pirouetting on one foot as he tried to open his umbrella under pouring rain, the overloaded basket dancing over his knee. Passersby giggling at the sight of the broken eggs, the lettuce head and tomatoes scattered all over the glistening pavement, a painterly scene, I thought. I'll never forget his frown and clenched features. I understood it all. The forgetfulness. The items missing from the list. I knew I had to stop nagging.

And weren't my mom's words prophetic? And her olden days rigmarole about men are like children—*they need to be praised*, and her same old tune about a man *not wanting a smarter wife*? Things don't change that easily. Nothing happens overnight. Think of the pond. What you really see is your own reflection, the reflection of your desires.

# Or Didn't She Tell You She's Been A Mother For Too Long?

And now with her children on their own, she plans their visits ahead rehearsing their favorite seafood dishes and entrées. She would set the table with candlelight, displaying the amethyst, turquoise, and moonstone grapes her husband once brought back from China. She remembers how she always prepared their baby food from scratch and misses nurturing them. To ensure the passing of time, she dreams of catching the waning crescent with a butterfly's net. She'd spoon feed its weakened light with a concoction spiked with crushed stars. Yes, she was an expert grinder, skilled in everything meant to please the palate.

# Or Have You Ever Noticed Erasure Patterns Within Fractals?

Scattered on a multi-faceted quilted pond, women's faces emerge, each as though from the center of a lotus about to drown before sunset. Eyes lined with kohl look alike. Their unanswered quest blurs the lines on the receding oval faces. In midst of that fractal fragmentation some hands stand out holding a blank sheet of paper, or were they once photographs of loved ones, so old the image was erased by indifference as life goes by with its dismembered seasons mixed pell-mell with gouache on that canvas like in a kaleidoscope constantly reshuffling its patterns, relying upon the onlooker to revisit the artist's gaze over the drowning faces.

.

IV.

## Or What If They Could Hear Each Other's Heartbeat?

With eyes shut, he sees through me
*will my bride's kiss be full of sweetness*
can I be that woman he wishes for
*sweetness sweeter than wine*
they say passion is a carmine flower
*I imagine her myrrh-scented hair*
soon red petals will stain my bed
*without having to say a word*
I shiver as a transparent leaf
*what if she feels my knees shaking*
does he dream of a red-haired courtesan
*we sat under the poplar's shade*
my body was anointed with musk
*the elders have gone to sleep*
where did all the violins go
*what if what lies behind her veil*
I wish tomorrow were yesterday
*we walked side by side in the olive grove*
I am a wingless dove caught in his arms
*I have scattered flowers under her steps*
how can I hide my budding chest

# Or How Did We Mend Failings With Golden Threads?

Has it always been that way?
*I am not sure what you mean*
Do you remember when we first met?
*People often said we looked alike*
Did you notice we both have an oval face?
*We also have a long nose and thin lips*
I could see myself reflected in your eyes
*I wanted to mold your vision into mine*
Don't we look alike more every day?
*I know what you are thinking right now*
We are sinking into a monochrome canvas
*I hold your hand and feel it is my own*
How did we tailor our dreams to fit?
*We've mastered the art of reconciliation*
You measure the right amount of spices
*Not even an emperor's palate is so refined*
I see your smile with memory's eyes
*I redress your arched back with one glance*
We've crafted selective memories
*Mended failings with golden threads*
To celebrate half a century of caring

# Or What Is Life If Not A Constant Carving Of Oneself?

And isn't happiness a matter
of instants, each a dance between
chi and chaos, a flux and reflux, a tidal
wave, rising and receding?

And aren't joy and sadness part
of the same equation, a fluid oscillation,
forward/backward?

Watch how the sand we write upon
only scars for a moment. Water
soothes, erases memories, a way to wash
away our passage on earth.

In the backyard of my mind
life passes like a meandering stream,
water carries silt,

licks riverbeds, tastes new shores,
gathers remnants of words
grain by grain, bit by bit, sharp-edged
syllables that smell of loss.

Let's get drunk on dew at dawn,
watch how oleander glows
under the blushing light.

# Or Don't We Often Need An *Allegro Ma Non Troppo*?

Think of a boy lost in midst
   of a rippling sound wave still
      hanging from his umbilical cord
   he lands on a tipsy summer moon
who tries to chase away the shadows
   from last night's hangover
      the boy wants to catch
his own shadow with a fisherman's
   pole that is really
      a violinist's bow

      A page has been turned  there's a gap
   in the  symphony

The boy waves his bow around
   a dragonfly and a pink-lipped orchid
      he wants to become
      *The Little Prince*
   get closer to the orchid's heart
but she is only pursing her lips for a kiss
      he envies the dragonfly's dance

      Another page  turned  another gap

   Spiritual fires rise out of darkness
in the moon's secret landscapes
   the dragonfly hides under its shadow
      the orchid sleeps awaiting a kiss
the boy knows he needs to keep in touch
   with his own shadow and will only
      hear its music with eyes closed
to find out where he came from
   and what he wants to become

## Or How Did I Even Think I'd Make It Back In Time For Class?

I'm late for class. I take a trolley but the old driver takes us
to a strange place by the beach. The sea and sky merge in clear
aquamarine. We watch a fisherman throw nets at a distance.
A boat ride would be lovely.

A girl in a flowered dress bends over a net of algae. I know her
but can't remember her name. She went to school with me in Cairo.
Tiny blue crabs crawl on the sand. On the rocky reefs, purple sea
urchins are nested. My Nonna loved to eat them in Alexandria,
*ricci, ricci,* she'd say with a smile.

We come across a stand. Smoke rises from ears of corn roasting
over coals. Oil, lemon, herbs, drizzle over tender flesh. It is getting
dark. Blue sparks electrify the dense air. I love the crab's orange
heart. It tastes just like in Rass el Bar, that little island where the Nile
blends with the Mediterranean. Vendors carried them in baskets,
chanting *kabouria! kabouria!*

It is time for cocktails. People gather around a buffet erected
at the foot of the cliff. They keep coming out of a transparent
elevator sliding in midst of the quartz sandstone. I think of a
fisherman's net rising with its catch. It could be our only way out.
It stops midway, a door opens to a conference room.

I see an old date from Beirut: an ophthalmologist with black
curly hair, still handsome. How does he manage to keep his hair
so black, so curly after forty years? I realize it is past nine.
How did I ever think I'd make it back in time for class?

# Or How Could I Find My Way In Suspension In Midst Of A Clearing?

Lying down on the grass
        eyes filled with kaleidoscopic
                images rolling at full speed:
the rabbit pulls me through
        a bottomless pit,
the red-breasted blackbird keeps
        whispering, do not look back,
                do not search for his deep eyes,
nevermore, nevermore.

The passerine's monotonous chant sways
        me away from the moment
                he holds my hand. I think of maps
of love still eluding me:
        they put flowers on my hair,
 sew dresses that mark my waistline,
        someday, someday, they'd say,
                won't forgive my drowning within
labyrinthine paths of wonder.

They want me to grow into a likeness
        their sight has already framed,
                keep me in a cocoon never imagining
my flight: weren't they ever lost in midst
        of a clearing or ever torn between
mirrors, I wonder, as I spend time
        chiseling my features and figure
                a curve here, a straighter line over there
attentive to the signals of my heartbeat.

I am still dizzy from falling
         flapping wings ground me
                  insisting eyes watch me from a balcony
I draw a *Map of Tendre* of every time
         he looks at me: didn't he whistle once
when I walked home carrying baguettes?
         And the other day, oblivious
                  of his friends, didn't he turn around
his glance piercing the nape of my neck?

Signs fill my pages awaiting to be
         deciphered: the flowers on my hair
                  feel heavier, their perfume weighs me
down, the rabbit is out of sight,
         the red-breasted blackbird keeps
                  chanting his rhythmic threnody

# Or Who Would Have Expected Us To Leave That Way?

We decided to skip the afternoon bus ride
and sneak out through the convent's main gate
guarded by the twin Sisters.

As soon as the hunchback nun turned around
to answer her stuttering twin's call from inside
the parlor, we jumped in unison

out the first floor's half-opened window.
We barely caught our breath till we reached
the town square.

We knew we couldn't remain unnoticed for long
in our gray uniform. At the sight of the juggler,
we stood, mesmerized.

His hands handled fiery balls in elliptical
trajectories bringing forth the movement
of stars and constellations.

The same energy flowed through our body
as we held hands tightly as though a single
cape enveloped us.

We had  become a vessel about to set sail.
Our philosophy professor, a Steve MacQueen
look-alike Jesuit,

seemed to be now wearing that juggler's black
hat matching his cassock. His hands spinning
faster and faster,

tossing blinding lights binding us as one.
All questions
            raised in class
                        burst into sparks.

# Or Would She Ever Shed Her Many Faces?

She searches for an aperture
to gather sunrays
on which she runs
her fingers,
listens to the mute music rise,
curl into a sparrow's song.
Lapis lazuli brushed over
eyelids lined with kohl
curve into the Eye of Horus,
land in the midst of a palm.

*Follow the course of rivers and rivulets, sense the echoes of dreams,*
*trap them in a net, hide them inside a Havana box filled with down,*
*then weave them into the many faces buried within you!*

Warned against stagnant waters,
she awaits the right time
to capture the moon's
nascent reflection,
knows she has to cross this threshold,
unite all masks collected
in deepest darkness,
espouse her shadow,
contemplate her unquenched thirst
without drowning.

*Yours must be an inner vision not a mere sight, you could not withstand*
*facing what you bear within! Like a midwife, go on delivering dreams*
*and illusions, don't worry if yours aren't fulfilled!*

Her mirror grows into a pond,
        a deep well reveals
veiled shapes
                shedding
gilded gowns, one by one.
        She slips in lunar light,
                hangs onto its asperities,
        climbs mountains
with seven-league boots,
        soars without wings.

*Unspoken words project shadows shaping their own dance, muffled echoes bring things to pass! Carve an alphabet legible only by you, add colors to your music! Remember you're only playing for yourself!*

# Or How Did You Think She'd Rehearse Her Own Flight?

A dissonant note rises
        silenced with
                colored threads.
Under deft fingers,
        two figures hide
        in the folds
of the cloth,
woven in an embrace,
        stitch by stitch,
as she rehearses her own flight.

She hasn't met him yet,
        but knows
                what he looks like.
Wasn't he tailor-made,
stitch by stitch,
        to fit her needs?
        Furtively, they fall
                head upside down,
in a cascade of fabric,
spill out
        the slit windows,
disappear into the landscape.

# Or Had She Told Him, Would He Have Understood?

*Tu étais fait à la taille de mon corps même*
—Marguerite Duras, *Hiroshima mon amour*


She could have told him,
like Emmanuelle Riva,
who thought she would
never experience
such passion again
"How could I know you'd fit
my body like a glove,"
but would he have understood?

She suddenly felt the deep
echoes of that woman's feelings,
first heard from an actress
in Alain Resnais's black and
white movie she'd seen when
she was too young to know
the language of bodies,
experience the tightness
of a custom-made garment
fitting like a fruit and its skin.

Eyes closed, she sinks
at times into the hollow well
of memory, her body comes
alive from every pore,
awakens sleeping butterflies
opening their wings at once,
folded wings that were
gateways, shadowy
interstices that kept hidden
memory and desire.

## Or What If They Could Only Coexist As An Artifact?

All that was left of the bridge was its armature
            a steel skeleton stripped of discarded feelings

        so many deep wants could no longer be fulfilled
only an artist's brush would fill the gaping gaps

no need to keep recounting virtues or flaws
            or reimagine a score made of fallen notes

        no need for each of them to keep appearances
or explore the itinerary of their dreams

let them be bare at last reveal their armature
            eviscerate themselves to unearth deep-rooted

        veins rewire them into coils no other men or
women espoused before stilted but much freer

            they'd need to visit Berrien's wire sculptures display
and see stillness in motion flow through hollowness

# Or What Did You Think Would Happen After You Were Gone?

There are times when even the sky feels like a ceiling preventing flights from the mind

There are times when drapes attempt to escape the window frame only to be pinned by an arrow aimed at a bird clothed in purple murex

There are times when sleeping on the deck of an abandoned wreck isn't the utmost homelessness

There are times when we need to listen to the language of fabrics and strive to stay away from desolate gray

There are times when objects are taking over a landscape where there is no one left to talk to

## Or Did You Really Think It Was The Path Of No Return?

When we started walking along the winding road
of separation, did you ever wonder if our shadows
weren't reluctant to follow?

What if they'd reclaim a life of their own,
decide to concoct a different ending to our story,
loosen their chains one by one?

What if they might have stretched and stretched,
retracing our footsteps towards the place where
words were last spoken or omitted?

And what if then, without restraint, without shame,
pride aside, they would have wrapped themselves
around each other in swirls tighter than the twists

of a rope, become braided wicks awaiting to be lit,
linger back there with no witness save, perhaps,
an alley cat, a stray dog, or a lost sparrow?

V.

# Or Why Do I Fast-Forward Lovers' Encounters On TV Shows?

What are elusive lovers if not erratic paths, mediocrity encountered at every major crossing when we get lost as we try to hold on tight to the wheel of fortune, lest it bends on the other side, tree stumps on which to stop and rest for a while, hoping they'll grow into a maple, or an oak, become strong enough so that we could stretch a hammock between their branches, rest while reading, swayed by the wind humming Aeolian tunes, maybe find a shoulder to help cross a stream of discontent or uncertainty, a staff, a shaft, a wooden crutch once meant to grow twigs bearing buds but instead dries up and breaks under our weight as an illusory axis mundi? What of the inanity of such quest, of attempting to create with a deck of cards a story, our story, the way some weave fleeting tales with Tarots, aligning them in vertical or horizontal lines, inventing new signs and symbols.

## Or Have You Ever Wondered Why She Is Looking Back?

Hoping to make sense of the artist's strokes,
the model sees the nape of her neck turn into
an unexpected dawn rising between her gathered
tresses and the low-cut black velvet dress.

Was he aware of the time spent applying the right
amount of eye shadow, a slight outline of kohl
and a touch of mascara? She even barely brushed
some blush over her lips, a natural look he favors.

And yet, her face is left offstage as the brushstrokes
add light to her naked back above the ruffled décolleté.
She watches the grain of skin sparkle like sand dunes
under midday sun, and drowns her sight within
the shaded area where so much is left unsaid.

# Or What If She Imagined He Loved Her Just That Once?

What if she'd slip into a dark pool, cross
    the mirror of her own
          pleasure, explore herself
from within, dive undressed
      in its depth next
to a body she could not forget?

What if she imagined it all just that once,
    synapses caught
         in silken webs spun by their lips,
a touch that splits minutes
       when he slid between her thighs
as naturally as a handshake?

*Ready to throw themselves into the waterfall,*
    *they held on to each other, in search for a center.*

What if each would become a part of a whole
    and she'd say, you have touched my soul,
        and meant it though she didn't have a clue
as to what a soul was, just sensed
      the tip of an invisible blue flame

burning along her spine as his skin
    unraveled under her fingertips?

What if she had found the key to the door
    opening dams in this dream
      within a dream?
Some say nothing is real without words
    to give it flesh

    and yet he never uttered a word
and neither did she, since it was what it was.

## Or Do We Ever Learn To Find The Key To Our Own Scribbling?

We jot down sparse lines to forget words spewed out like fire breathing plumes, try to erase our trails, kneel down, wiping each footstep with long bristles as we move forward. By erasing traces so well, we no longer recognize our own, and watch how signs run as rivers branching out in streams, echoed here and there throughout the pages.

Like a gold digger following veins embedded as threads within quartz rock or disseminated in silicified limestone we scan our lives, turn the hour hand to unearth leitmotivs, dilating encounters steeped in deep blue, frozen within a cave or a basement, a mansard or an attic hoarding our dreams. Bent over our own reflection, we crawl like infants to find the crumbs left at our passage.

## Or Have You Ever Heard Of A Cipher Even Freud Couldn't Elucidate?

It could be a seal
        carved in
flesh
its winding lines
             like fingerprints
        or tree rings
            in a sawn trunk
marking a threshold
in red ink
        or blood

            A written language
tattooed in defiance
        of finding its key

A seal that raises the notion
        of trespassing
or
colonizing
        in the name of desire

An intricate barrier
        not meant to be ignored
            but understood
        not to be toppled
but deconstructed

        And doesn't history
record how
        it often takes a woman
            to unwind
the thread?

# Or What If Scars Would Suddenly Become Translucent?

*I wish that I could show you when you are lonely or in darkness*
*the astonishing light of your own being.*
—Hafez

Did the Persian poet mean that it would
take a special viewer to perceive the
truth within? We were taught to hide our
sorrow, forget and store grief in drawers.

We learned to cover our imperfections
with makeup, and disappointments under
a smile. We showcased our very best
with trompe l'oeil pleated skirts.

Wouldn't the art of concealing allow
pain to grow insidiously, preventing
the mind from exploring one's rocky
shores and inner landscapes?

Page Bradley re-membered the broken
shards of a nude woman's sculpture seated
in a lotus position. At night, a light
radiates from its core through seam lines.

Each crack, a lightning. A victory.
The way Japanese *kintsukuroi*
mends fragments of a broken vessel
with gold. The repairing of shattered
tesserae expressing hurt as renewal.

And what if invisible scars reclaimed
their corporeality by being tattooed
all over the body or materialize through
translucent crevices letting light out,
revealing the archeology of pain?

# Or What I Really Do When You Think I'm Knitting

I think of so many doors that were once closed and opened, of
all the doors I wish to reopen. My breath espouses the clicking
of needles, I count three for a hole, skip a thread for a gap, loops
form ephemeral ripples, a wish gone sour, a sunken coin.

At times, I'll erase an entire row, move patterns backwards, relive
the moment I crawled into the warmth of my parents' bed. In my
old grey Shetland shawl, you know, the one wrapped around my
shoulders, lie all the emotions, designs, I would ever recreate.

With each lace hole, sorrow melts a ruffled feather, a caress my
fingertips long for, or did you think my back was always bent,
hands knotted? Rows of holes form a river that wanders without
leaving its bed, a bed of Queen Anne's Lace spreads over the eyes
of my skin wounded by the scent of wildflowers.

Memories morph into delicate configurations conjured up as
I purse my lips in concentration: my heart bursts in my chest
like a ripe pomegranate under noon's sun. Under my tongue a
hummingbird flutters at the twitch of each stitch, each stitch a scar.
I play Solitaire with yarn and needle, shuffle and reshuffle at will.

# Or Can't You Hear The Harshness Of Her Breath?

Seated in the corner of a room lit by a dim light, she tries to
stitch her past anew: her deft fingers set on insufflating life by
interlocking fibers. Her failed attempts, a museum of limp
figures, face faceless couples hanging from the walls while
her cat, once thought to be her masterpiece, unravels himself
playfully into a ball of black yarn unaware of his waning
existence.

She'd sit for hours as the click of the needles would follow a
rhythm of its own till she understood the need for change. At
dusk, she inhaled deeply out of the open window and spun yarn
with the shades of night

> *muffled notes, motes of dust flown from dark alleys,*
> *people's breath and clothes, the slightest waft*
> *bearing plumes, dandelions seeds' tufted tops, pappi,*
> *broken fireflies' elytra, cottonwood fluff, thistledown,*
> *milkweed, all the stuff birds collect to build their nests.*

As patterns became her cipher, the movement of the needles
intensified as that of someone typing nonstop on a keyboard. An
automaton, she suffers sanguine wounds with every stitch while
the stained garment becomes corporeal, colors her alter ego in
red, turns into a silhouette that escapes her grasp shedding ashen
layers as from a worn out shroud.

# Or How Can Woven Whispers Be Deciphered?

                   What do such repetitive patterns mean,
        inserted visual poems,            wordless speech
lost in a scarf or a shawl, shaded emotions
hiding under every motif,       inside every angle,
                an echo of Philomela's cries bursting in silence,
each colored thread telling     of the outrage,
of a beauty flawed, of a body no longer hers,
        of a tongue severed as        a trembling stem.
            See how carmine blood runs thick
between her thighs,     down her throat,
suffocating her.  Only deft fingers would feel
        the softness or ruggedness     of each fiber
           and weave relentless nightmares, whispering
night after night         against the darkness.

# Or When Brushstrokes Dance In Concentric Circles

When after a heavy rain, nature's prism refracts light,
juxtaposed colors seem to coexist peacefully within
an invisible threshold, the way an elderly couple stays
close while protecting unspoken boundaries.

The artist makes the rainbow swirl wild over the canvas
as a conductor raising his wand through colored patterns'
rhythms, creating occasional collisions. Broken dialogues
reveal angles replete with hidden whispers.

Rainbows form and disperse around the seated couple:
he listens to music while she daydreams, hand resting
on a stack of old books. She caresses each spine trying
to remember a few opening lines.

When they break the silence, speech overlaps as they
change the subject and let it recur in circles. Sentences
run over a circumference then circle back around smaller
and smaller circles.

Back to the center of an unanswered question.

# Or Why Would Anyone Want To Draw A Keyhole?

This is not the outline
of a silhouette.

I am drawing a keyhole
to find my way
out of my own cell.

This is the black silk
thread spun by the ink
brush rising out
of sweat and blood.

# Or Did You Think I'd Never Find The Way Out?

It took me a while
        to wake up from
                a life not lived

        I'd lost count of hours
lying on a bed of algae

not an Ophelia
        by vocation
                I tear open

        my silk shirt
free my mind from layers

of false pretense

        the sound of a voice
                startles me
                        with words

        strange as a shooting
star landing on my lap

walking through
        endless corridors

I open door after
                door after door

find myself
        squeezed within
each paneling

as though framed
                within my past
                        in a sur place
pasodoble solo

            one step forward
another backwards

            I move in the dense
                air as in a dry
                        aquarium

the last door faces
            a mirror outlining
                    a woman
I never knew

# List of Art and Visuals Used as Inspiration

"Or Am I Or Am I Not A Knot Of Contradictions?" *Harmony* by Remedios Varo

"Or Aren't Words Worthless, Oftentimes Said & Forgotten, Written & Erased?" *Beyond Words* by Liz Collins

"Or Call Me A Hoarder If You Will But Try To Understand," *Harmony*, by Remedios Varo

"Or Can't You See How They All Stare At Us Even The Birds Resting On Their Hands?" *The Immigrants' Boat* by Marilene Sawaf

"Or Can't You See How We're Weaving Ourselves Tight?" *Three Women and Three Owls* by Juanita Guccione

"Or Can't You Hear The Harshness Of Her Breath?" *The Red Weaver* by Remedios Varo

"Or Can't You See That We Want Our Voices To Be Heard?" Photographs of the Lebanon Protests, October 17, 2019

"Or Can't You See What We've Become Through The Half-Open Door?" *Ceremonia* by Fernando de Szyszlo

"Or Could I Finally Be Allowed To Leave My Analyst?" *Woman Leaving the Psychoanalyst* by Remedios Varo

"Or Could There Ever Be Rainbows In Midst Of A Storm?" *Syrian Migration #9* by Helen Zughaib

"Or Didn't She Tell You She's Been A Mother For Too Long?" *Celestial Pablum* by Remedios Varo

"Or Didn't You Know It's In That Opening & Closing That We Exist?" *Icon* by Remedios Varo

"Or Didn't You Know That What You Really See Is Your Own Reflection?" *Young Husband: First Marketing* by Lilly Martin Spencer

"Or Did You Ever See The Other Side Of Things?" *Disturbing Presence* by Remedios Varo

"Or Did You Ever Wonder What It's Like To Have Hot Flashes?" *The Souls of the Mountain* by Remedios Varo

"Or Did You Think Crushed Hopes Couldn't Reawaken?" *Spring Flight* by Helen Zughaib

"Or Did You Think I'd Never Find The Way Out?" *Birthday,* by Leonora Carrington

"Or Did You Really Think It Was The Path Of No Return?" *The Farewell* by Remedios Varo

"Or Don't Be Fooled By Her Self-Righteousness," *De lo eterno y lo lúdico* by Cristina Francov

"Or Don't You Ever Offer Yourself As A Main Course," *Unexpected Visit* by Remedios Varo

"Or Don't We Often Need An *Allegro Ma Non Troppo?*" *Four Symphonies (# III)* by Wadada Leo Smith

"Or Had She Told Him, Would He Have Understood?" After the movie, *Hiroshima mon amour*, directed by Alain Resnais, screenplay by Marguerite Duras

"Or Have You Ever Heard Of A Cipher Even Freud Couldn't Elucidate?" *The Labyrinth of Venus* by Ana Mendieta

"Or Have You Ever Noticed Erasure Patterns Within Fractals?" *Generations Lost* by Helen Zughaib

"Or Have You Ever Wondered Why She Is Looking Back?" *A Backward Glance* by Charles Edward Perugini

"Or How A Lover's Skin Shivers Like Moonlight Over Water," *Insomnia* by Remedios Varo

"Or How Can We Ever Cut Down To The Bare Essentials?" *The Vagabond* by Remedios Varo

"Or How Can Woven Whispers Be Deciphered?" *Women Against the Night* by Helen Zughaib

"Or How Could I Find My Way In Suspension In Midst Of A Clearing?" *Madeline Series* by Marilene Sawaf

"Or How Could He Ever Win The Heart Of Any Woman?" *Dead Leaves* by Remedios Varo

"Or How Could We Ever Be Able To Resist Such Likeness?" *The Way the Wind Blows* by Juanita Guccione

"Or How Did We Mend Failings With Golden Threads?" *Lovers* by Remedios Varo

"Or How Did You Think She'd Rehearse Her Own Flight?" *Embroidering the Earth's Mantle* by Remedios Varo

"Or How Do You Keep Track Of All The Keys You Once Owned?" *Keys* by Shiharu Shiota

"Or How Do You Think We Came To Be Stranded In That No-Man's-Land?" Surrealistic paintings by Salvador Dalí, Kay Sage, Yves Tanguy, Gertrude Abercrombie and René Magritte.

"Or How Long Do You Think She Could Keep It Up Without Falling?" *The Shining One* by Salma Caller

"Or How Much Of Yourself Remains Within The Walls Of A Home?" *Salt Marsh* by Jeremy Miranda

"Or How With Each Dream She'd Feel Closer To The Receding Shoreline," *Salvation* by Kara Williams

"Or Isn't The Cat The Only Sensible Being In That Painting?" *In The Distance* by Andrea Kowch

"Or Weren't We Always Told To Remove Our Makeup At Night?" *After She Had Many Faces* by Juanita Guccione

"Or Weren't You Ever Told That Nothing Comes Out Of Nothing?" *A Dream* by Wadada Leo Smith

"Or What Did You Expect, An Eternal Status Quo?" *Underwater Sculptures* by Jason deCaires Taylor

"Or What Did You Think Would Happen After You Were Gone?" *Catalogue Raisonné* by Kay Sage

"Or What Does A Tree Know About Aging?" *Ancient Trees Series* by Beth Moon

"Or What Else Could We Do But Raise Our Hands?" *Arabesque Mortem* by Reem Bassous

"Or What I Really Do When You Think I'm Knitting," *Mademoiselle Boissière Knitting* by Gustave Caillebotte

"Or What If One Could Overhear Words Hovering Over A Pond?" *Encounter* by Remedios Varo

"Or What If Scars Would Suddenly Become Translucent?" *Expansion* by Paige Bradley

"Or What If She'd Chosen To Drown In A River Of Down?" *White Ophelia* by Joanna Smielowska

"Or What If They Could Hear Each Other's Heartbeat?" *Bride under the Canopy* by Marc Chagall

"Or What If They Could Only Coexist As An Artifact?" Wire Sculptures by Elizabeth Berrien

"Or What If You Could Overhear Our Hushed Voices?" *Horse, Owl and Chaise* by Gertrude Abercrombie; *Horses series* by Xu Beihong

"Or What's In A Bird's Song, Unraveled?" *Creation of The Birds* by Remedios Varo

"Or What's In An Inverted Image?" *Pacifica* by Wadada Leo Smith

"Or Who Would Have Expected Us To Leave That Way?" *The Juggler* by Remedios Varo

"Or When Brushstrokes Dance In Concentric Circles," *Electric Prisms* by Sonia Delauney

"Or Why Would Anyone Want To Draw A Keyhole?" *Red Balance* by Wadada Leo Smith

"Or Would It Have Made A Difference, Had I Known?" *The Bride* by Safia Farhat

"Or Would She Ever Shed Her Many Faces?" *Born Again* by Remedios Varo

# Notes

"Or What If They Could Only Coexist As An Artifact?" (p. 68) is a Singaporean Found/Fount Sonnet. The base text is Italo Calvino's *Invisible Cities*, translated by William Weaver (p. 15); with the fourteen found words as follows: armature, of, wants, the, virtues, of, each, itinerary, be, to, men, but, visit, and.

The Singaporean sonnet, invented by editor Desmond Kon Zhicheng-Mingdé, comprises the 14 lines expected of any sonnet, while dipping into existing texts to unearth 14 distinct words, each of which are then woven into each of the 14 lines. Fragments of historical or literary texts are invoked, as pivots around which envelop the lyric of the new poem. This method is borne of Oulipo aesthetics.

HEDY HABRA is a poet, artist and essayist. She is the author of four poetry collections from Press 53 including *The Taste of the Earth* (2019), winner of the 2020 Silver Nautilus Book Award, honorable mention for the Eric Hoffer Book Award, and finalist for the Best Book Award. Her second collection, *Under Brushstrokes*, was finalist for the 2015 USA Best Book Award and the International Book Award, and her first poetry collection, *Tea in Heliopolis*, won the 2014 USA Best Book Award and was finalist for the International Book Award. Her story collection, *Flying Carpets*, won the 2013 Arab American National Book Award's honorable mention and was finalist for the 2014 Eric Hoffer Award and the USA Best Book Award. Her book of literary criticism, *Mundos alternos y artísticos en Vargas Llosa* (2012), explores the visual and interartistic elements in the Peruvian Nobel Laureate's fiction. Habra holds a B.S. in Pharmacy. She earned an M.A. and an M.F.A. in English and an M.A. and Ph.D. in Spanish literature, all from Western Michigan University where she has been teaching. A recipient of the Nazim Hikmet Poetry Award, she won honorable mention from *Tiferet* and was finalist for *Nimrod*'s Pablo Neruda Award. A twenty-one-time nominee for the Pushcart Prize and Best of the Net, her work has been translated into Arabic, Mandarin, Spanish and Turkish. Her multilingual work appears in numerous journals and anthologies, including *Aeolian Harp Series*, *The Bitter Oleander*, *California Quarterly*, *Cider Press Review*, *Cimarron Review*, *Connotation Press*, *Cutthroat*, *The Cortland Review*, *Diode*, *The Ekphrastic Review*, *Feral*, *Gargoyle*, *The MacGuffin*, *MacQueen's Quarterly*, *MAYDAY*, *MockingHeart Review*, *New York Quarterly*, *Nimrod*, *The Opiate*, *Peacock Journal*, *Panoplyzine*, *Poet Lore*, *Pirene's Fountain*, *SLANT*, *Solstice*, *Tiferet*, *Valparaiso Poetry Review*, *Verse Daily*, *Vox Populi*, and *World Literature Today*. Her website is HedyHabra.com

Printed in the USA
CPSIA information can be obtained
at www.ICGtesting.com
JSHW022055121023
50071JS00004B/167

9 781950 413690